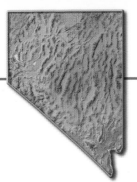

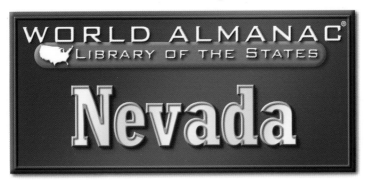

WORLD ALMANAC®
LIBRARY OF THE STATES

Nevada

THE SILVER STATE

by Jon Hana

WORLD ALMANAC® LIBRARY

Please visit our web site at: www.worldalmanaclibrary.com
For a free color catalog describing World Almanac® Library's list of high-quality books and multimedia programs, call 1-800-848-2928 (USA) or 1-800-387-3178 (Canada). World Almanac® Library's fax: (414) 332-3567.

Library of Congress Cataloging-in-Publication Data available upon request from publisher. Fax (414) 336-0157 for the attention of the Publishing Records Department.

ISBN 0-8368-5154-4 (lib. bdg.)
ISBN 0-8368-5325-3 (softcover)

First published in 2003 by
World Almanac® Library
330 West Olive Street, Suite 100
Milwaukee, WI 53212 USA

A Creative Media Applications Production
Design: Alan Barnett, Inc.
Copy editor: Laurie Lieb
Fact checker: Joan Verniero
Photo researcher: Jamey O'Quinn
World Almanac® Library project editor: Tim Paulson
World Almanac® Library editors: Mary Dykstra, Gustav Gedatus, Jacqueline Laks Gorman, Lyman Lyons
World Almanac® Library art direction: Tammy Gruenewald
World Almanac® Library graphic designers: Scott M. Krall, Melissa Valuch

Photo credits: pp. 4-5 © Galen Rowell/CORBIS; p. 6 (top right) © Buddy Mays/CORBIS; p. 6 (bottom right) © David A. Northcott/CORBIS; p. 6 (left) © Anthony Cooper; Ecoscene/CORBIS; p. 7 (top) © AP/Wide World Photos; p. 7 (bottom) © Thomas Wiewandt; Visions of America/CORBIS; p. 9 © Ted Streshinsky/CORBIS; p. 10 © Arthur Rothstein/CORBIS; p. 11 © Hulton Archive/Getty Images; p. 12 © CORBIS; p. 13 © Hulton Archive/Getty Images; p. 14 © Michael Keller/CORBIS; p. 15 (top) © AP/Wide World Photos; p. 15 (bottom) © AP/Wide World Photos; p. 17 © Travel Nevada; p. 18 © Richard Cummins/CORBIS; p. 19 © Scott T. Smith/CORBIS; p. 20 (left) © Royalty-Free/CORBIS; p. 20 (center) © Palmer/Kane, Inc./CORBIS; p. 20 (right) © Travel Nevada; p. 21 (left) © David Muench/CORBIS; p. 21 (center) © Royalty-Free/CORBIS; p. 21 (right) © Scott T. Smith/CORBIS; p. 23 © Kennan Ward/CORBIS; p. 26 © PictureNet/CORBIS; p. 27 © Raymond Gehman/CORBIS; p. 29 © Travel Nevada; p. 31 © AP/Wide World Photos; p. 32 © Scott T. Smith/CORBIS; p. 33 © Morton Beebe/CORBIS; p. 34 © Mark E. Gibson/CORBIS; p. 35 © Jan Butchofsky-Houser/CORBIS; p. 36 © Travel Nevada; p. 37 (top) © AP/Wide World Photos; p. 37 (bottom) © AP Photo/Lennox McLendon; p. 38 © AP/Wide World Photos; p. 39 © Nevada Historical Society; p. 41 (left) © AP/Wide World Photos; p. 41 (right) © AP/Wide World Photos; pp. 42-43 © Hulton Archive/Getty Images; p. 44 (top) © Jan Butchofsky-Houser/CORBIS; p. 44 (bottom) © Travel Nevada; p. 45 (top) © AP/Wide World Photos; p. 45 (bottom) © Travel Nevada

Printed in the United States of America

3 4 5 6 7 8 9 09 08 07 06 05

Nevada

Blossoming Desert

Nevada is the fastest growing state in the nation. The rugged beauty of Nevada is truly awe inspiring. Most of the state lies on a wide highland between the Sierra Nevada mountain range and the Rocky Mountains. The diverse landscape features sandy deserts with cactus and grayish-green sagebrush, snow-peaked mountains, steep valleys, and pine forests. Hot springs and geysers shoot up from the rocky land. Nevada's natural beauty forms a backdrop to a number of thriving service, manufacturing, and mining industries.

Tourism is Nevada's biggest service industry, and entertainment and gambling are big attractions for state visitors. Nevada's gambling casinos, most of which are located in the cities of Las Vegas, Lake Tahoe, and Reno, are famous for their luxurious hotels and fine nightclubs. Beautiful Lake Tahoe is located in a valley in the mountains of the Sierra Nevada. This giant lake is popular for swimming and boating in summer. In winter, skiers take to the nearby slopes.

Nevada's most popular nickname is the Silver State, because huge amounts of silver were found and mined there in the nineteenth and early twentieth centuries. At the time of the discovery, miners rushed to the state to find their fortunes. Mining is still an important industry, and gold and silver, along with many other minerals, are found in Nevada, where sites of mining history are another popular tourist attraction. Ghost towns and mining towns also draw many visitors.

Nevada is a hot and dry state, but its agriculture industry uses a system of irrigation to grow crops such as wheat, alfalfa seed, and hay. In the central and eastern regions of the state, ranchers raise sheep and cattle. In recent years, manufacturers have flocked to the state because of its favorable tax laws. Nevada has been, and continues to be, an example of American ingenuity, determination, and imagination.

► Map of Nevada showing the interstate highway system, as well as major cities and waterways.

▼ A road winds through Nevada's sparsely inhabited yet surprisingly picturesque, desert terrain.

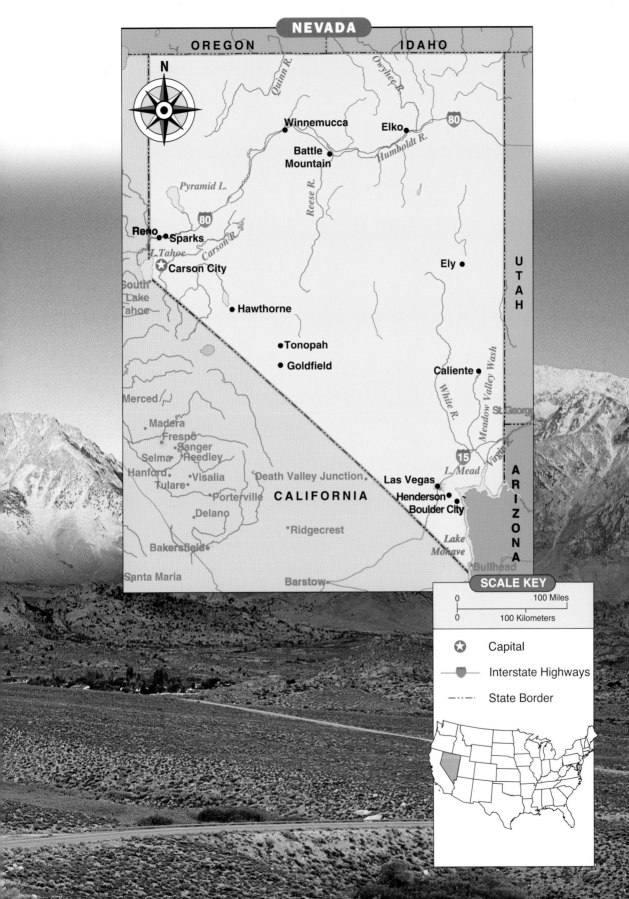

NEVADA

OREGON — IDAHO

N

Quinn R.
Owyhee R.

Winnemucca
Elko
80

Battle
Mountain
Humboldt R.

Pyramid L.
Reese R.

80

Reno
Sparks
L.Tahoe
Carson R.

Carson City

Ely

South
Lake
Tahoe

Hawthorne

•Tonopah

• Goldfield

Caliente

White R.

Meadow Valley Wash

Merced

Madera
Fresno
Sanger
Selma Reedley
Hanford
Tulare Visalia

St George

15

Death Valley Junction

Las Vegas
L. Mead
Virgin R.

CALIFORNIA

Henderson
Boulder City

A
R
I
Z
O
N
A

Porterville

Delano

•Ridgecrest

Lake Mohave

Bakersfield

Santa Maria

Barstow•

Bullhead

U
T
A
H

SCALE KEY

0   100 Miles

0   100 Kilometers

⭐ Capital

▬ Interstate Highways

–··– State Border

Fast Facts

Nevada (NV), The Silver State, The Sagebrush State, The Battle Born State

Entered Union

October 31, 1864 (36th state)

Capital   **Population**

Carson City 52,457

Total Population (2000)

1,998,257 (35th most populous state) — *Between 1990 and 2000, the state's population increased 66.3 percent.*

Largest Cities   **Population**

Las Vegas 478,434
Paradise 186,070
Reno 180,480
Henderson 175,381
Sunrise Manor 156,120

Land Area

109,826 square miles (284,449 square kilometers) (7th largest state)

State Motto

"All for Our Country"

State Song

"Home Means Nevada," *words and music by Bertha Raffetto, adopted in 1933.*

State Animal

Desert bighorn sheep

State Bird

Mountain bluebird

State Fish

Lahontan cutthroat trout

State Reptile

Desert tortoise

State Flower

Sagebrush

State Trees

Bristlecone pine, Single-leaf piñon

State Grass

Indian rice grass

State Metal

Silver

State Fossil

Ichthyosaur

State Colors

Silver and blue

State Artifact

Tule duck decoy — *Native Americans of Nevada made these duck decoys out of straw more than 2,000 years ago. Then hunters placed the decoys on lakes to attract real ducks, which the hunters would kill by throwing darts or stones.*

State Precious Gemstone

Black fire opal — *This rare gem is found in good quantity only in Nevada.*

State Rock

Sandstone — *The Carson City state capitol building is made of sandstone.*

Bowers Mansion, *Carson City*
Bowers Mansion is a large home built in 1864 to look like an old-style Italian villa. It was built by "Sandy" Bowers, a silver miner who struck it rich from the Comstock Lode.

Fleischmann Planetarium, *Reno*
Fleischmann Planetarium is located at the University of Nevada in Reno. It has a collection of realistic films about space adventures and about weather conditions, such as tornadoes and hurricanes.

Great Basin National Park
Great Basin National Park in east-central Nevada contains Wheeler Peak, limestone caves, and four-thousand-year-old bristlecone pines.

For other places and events, see p. 44.

BIGGEST, BEST, AND MOST

- Nevada has more hotel rooms than any other place in the world.
- Nevada is the largest producer of gold in the United States.
- The Hoover Dam, on the Colorado River, was the largest single public works project in U.S. history.

STATE FIRSTS

- **1858** The state's first newspaper, the *Territorial Enterprise,* hit the newsstands.
- **1918** Nevada's Anne Martin, a pacifist and women's rights activist, was the first woman ever to run for the U.S. Senate.
- **1931** The first gambling casino to open on the future Las Vegas Strip was the Pair-O-Dice Club.
- **1933** "Hard hats," helmets designed to protect the heads of construction workers, were invented for the workers who built the Hoover Dam.

Fish Story

It seems strange, but the dry, desert state of Nevada is home to two very rare fish. One is a very large sucker called the cui-ui. It is found only in Pyramid Lake and is considered endangered. Long ago, Native American peoples used cui-ui as a major food source. Another rare fish is the Devil's Hole pupfish, found only in the limestone caverns known as Devil's Hole in the southern Nevada desert. Prehistoric lakes dried up, leaving these species in isolated underwater caves, or sinks, where they developed separately from more common types of fish.

Wild Horses

Nevada is home to a large number of wild horses and mules. These herds are the legacy of Spanish explorers and cowboys, whose stray horses and mules survived in the wild over many generations. Herds of wild mustangs roam the Red Desert and Nevada's other wide open basins. Stallions fighting to gain the attention of mares in the herd are a common sight. The Wild Horse Preservation Commission of Nevada works to keep a healthy environment for the horses on the public lands of the state.

The Story of the Silver State

> After a day's journey of 18 miles . . .
> at a camping ground called Las Vegas . . .
> Two narrow streams of clear water, four or five feet deep,
> gush suddenly with a quick current, from two
> singularly large springs. . . . The taste of the water
> is good, but rather too warm to be agreeable,
> the temperature being 71 in the one and 73 in the other.
> They, however, afford a delightful bathing place.
>
> — *John C. Frémont's journal entry
> of May 3, 1843, describing his exploration of
> what is today the city of Las Vegas*

The ashes and bones of some of the earliest Native American peoples can still be found in present-day Nevada. The Natives of the Lovelock culture lived in Nevada between twelve thousand and twenty thousand years ago. They survived by fishing and hunting ducks. They painted memories of their cave-dwelling life on rocks throughout southern Nevada. Pueblo Indians were also among the first Native Americans in the area. The Pueblo Indians built their settlements along the Virgin and Muddy Rivers, near Las Vegas. They established a system of irrigation canals and built hive-like homes of sticks and mud. Their culture flourished for almost five hundred years.

When Europeans explored Nevada in the early 1800s, they encountered Washoe, Shoshone, Mohave, and Paiute. These Native Americans lived in large groups and often joined together for hunting or gathering food. During the winter months, these wandering groups settled in one place. They built houses made of poles covered by reeds or grass. Their lives were peaceful, full of celebration and religious tradition. Younger members of the Native groups played a game similar to soccer, and gambling games with tiny sticks for dice were also popular. The adults spent most of their free time gathering food to feed their people.

Native Americans of Nevada

- Mohave
- Paiute
- Shoshone
- Washoe

DID YOU KNOW?

Nevada got its name from a Spanish word that means "snowy." It refers to the mountain range called the Sierra Nevada, which means "snowy mountain range." Settlers in the area chose the name *Nevada* in 1861 when the area became a territory of the United States.

Exploration

Nevada was the last area of what is now the continental United States to be explored. Historians believe that in 1776 (the year the colonies declared independence from Britain), a Spanish missionary named Francisco Garcés may have been the first European to cross part of southern Nevada, passing through on his way from New Mexico to California. About fifty years later, in the 1820s, U.S. and British fur trappers and traders explored parts of Nevada. A trapper named Peter Skene Ogden, who worked for the Hudson's Bay Company, crossed what is currently the northern boundary of the state with a group of other trappers. Ogden used this route across the Humboldt River valley many times, trapping along the streams and rivers, but he never settled there.

An American trader named Jedediah Smith was the first white man to cross Nevada in 1826–1827. He led trappers across the Las Vegas valley region into California. Then he crossed back through the area called the Great Basin. Smith was followed in 1830 by William Wolfskill, who blazed a route named the Old Spanish Trail. It ran from Santa Fe, New Mexico, to Los Angeles, California, and opened a trade route to Nevada from the southeast. Next, Joseph Walker led other trappers along the Humboldt River to California in 1833. Walker and his men fought the first battle in Nevada between Native peoples and whites. The Native Americans had never before seen guns and lost about forty men in the skirmish. The trail Walker blazed was later used by wagons heading west to California during the Gold Rush in 1848.

From 1843 to 1845, John C. Frémont, with Kit Carson acting as his guide, explored the Great Basin and the mountains of the Sierra Nevada. He created the first detailed maps of the region. Frémont found and mapped the Carson River, which he named after his guide.

▼ A Shoshone woman sits beside her tepee in this period photo. The Western Shoshone of Nevada were mostly nomadic and joined other families only briefly for hunts or dancing.

Early Settlement

In 1848, as a result of a treaty to end the Mexican War, the United States acquired the Nevada region from Mexico. Nevada became part of the territory that included Utah, California, and land in parts of four other states. The first non-Native Nevada settlement was Dayton, settled by prospectors in 1849. That year, Brigham Young, leader of a religious order, the Church of Jesus Christ of Latter-Day Saints (called the Mormons), organized Utah, Nevada, and other land into a region he named the State of Deseret. Young wanted Congress to admit his land as a state of the Union. Congress refused and, instead, established Utah Territory in 1850, and Young was made governor. His followers settled in the new territory, and, in 1851, he built a trading post in Carson Valley, selling rations and supplies to prospectors heading to California to search for gold. The post was called Mormon Station (now Genoa). Other Mormons moved to the area, too, and began to ranch and raise livestock in Carson Valley. The area grew into what was called Carson County.

▼ This town that grew up around Mormon Station, now known as Genoa, was one of the first non-Native settlements in Nevada.

Conflict soon developed in Carson County. A minority of settlers didn't follow the Mormon religion and felt the Mormons, whose religious beliefs often clashed with the policies of government, were trying to live outside the law. This minority was opposed to being governed by the leader of the Mormon Church and petitioned Congress to separate Carson County from the Utah Territory and Young's control. When Congress refused to make changes, tension in the area increased. In 1857, fearing for the safety of his followers from non-Mormon settlers and government troops attempting to make peace in the area, Young moved the Mormon settlers east to Salt Lake City, Utah. The remaining settlers petitioned Congress to set up a temporary government in Carson City, but Congress refused, citing sparse population as its reason.

The Comstock Lode: "Strike It Rich!"

The history of Nevada changed abruptly in 1859, when the Comstock Lode, a rich deposit of silver ore, was discovered in present-day Virginia City. The discovery, named for Henry Comstock, a Nevada prospector, prompted hundreds to rush east from California to what is now Nevada, hoping to make their fortunes. Ironically, Comstock himself sold out too early and missed earning any substantial amount of money.

Virginia City quickly grew into a major center for mining. The miners lived a dangerous and difficult life in tents, caves, and huts made of stone. The settlements were lawless and often filled with suspect individuals. Mining was dangerous and costly work. Purchasing and transporting supplies across the mountains to Nevada was costly. The grueling work of silver mining consisted of chipping away at mountains to make shafts from which ore could be extracted. Working in dark tunnels they dug themselves, the prospectors stood in water up to their knees. There was real danger of a cave-in,

John C. Frémont

It has been said that John C. Frémont put Las Vegas on the map. This adventurer and explorer was born in Savannah, Georgia, in 1813. He was a brilliant but unruly student who was expelled from college. In 1837, when Frémont was hired by the federal government to survey parts of Georgia and the Carolinas, he traveled by pack mule. Frémont was then sent to map and explore the West. Working with the famous scout Kit Carson, he surveyed the area from 1843 to 1845. Frémont was the first explorer of Nevada to create a map of the region. More than twenty thousand copies of his map were immediately published and distributed to pioneers heading west through Nevada on their way to California. Because it was on the route shown on the map, Las Vegas became a major stopping point for travelers, where they picked up supplies for their trip.

in which the miners might be buried alive under tons of heavy rocks and dirt. For some, the effort paid off, and they made vast fortunes. Most miners did not.

Nevada Territory and Statehood

In March 1861, just before he left office, President James Buchanan declared Nevada separate from Utah. The population had swelled to more than fourteen thousand. Abraham Lincoln, who took office within days of Buchanan's order, appointed James W. Nye of New York City as governor of the new territory.

Before the new government of Nevada could be established, however, the Civil War began. President Lincoln knew that Nevadans were against slavery. Eager to increase support for the North in the war, Lincoln made Nevada into a new state. Technically, there were not enough residents for Nevada to qualify as a state, but Lincoln used executive

▼ Miners working 900 feet (274 meters) underground in a Virginia City mine, circa 1867. Many miners died from the heat or developed respiratory disease from inhaling rock dust.

privilege in declaring the nation's thirty-sixth state on October 31, 1864.

The first convention to adopt a state constitution failed, because the people of Nevada did not like the idea of taxing the state's mines, a plan that had been proposed by Congress. In September 1864, the voters approved a constitution written by a second convention. The people of Nevada elected a mining engineer named Henry G. Blasdel as their first state governor.

Mining: Recession and Recovery

Although the Comstock Lode was a rich silver deposit, many other mining sites in Nevada produced only a low-grade ore. These mines were still able to make a profit, however, because the government demand for silver was high. Then, in the early 1870s, the U.S. government decided to limit the amount of silver in its coins. Mines that produced low-grade ore failed. People lost their jobs, and thousands left Nevada to make a living elsewhere. Ghost towns — small cities that had once been thriving mining centers but now had no inhabitants — became a familiar sight.

The ranching industry began to grow as mining faded in importance. But the ranchers also had problems. To ship their livestock to other states, they were forced to pay the railroad very steep prices. Then, in the late 1880s, severely cold winters killed many cattle. Many small ranchers sold out to large cattle concerns.

Once again, however, good luck brought about the beginning of economic recovery in Nevada. In 1900, huge silver deposits were discovered in Tonopah. The silver was easy to mine and produced a greater profit than the low-grade ore. Other minerals, such as copper ore, were found near Ely. Then gold was located near Goldfield in 1902. Thousands of miners returned to Nevada. Economic recovery was under way.

Railroads were expanded into the mining areas so equipment could be more easily transported. This turned out to be useful for the cattle ranchers, who now had a more convenient, less expensive way to ship their livestock.

Agriculture also grew in the early 1900s when the Newlands Irrigation Project, the first federal irrigation plan, was begun. Dams were built along the Truckee and Carson Rivers to make reservoirs to irrigate crops and to provide electrical energy for the state. This irrigation system still supplies water to the west-central part of the state today.

▲ When Nevada became a state in 1864, its state legislature appointed James W. Nye, seen in this 1865 portrait, to the U.S. Senate. Nye served Nevada as a Senator until 1873.

Harold's Club

The first large casino in Nevada was Harold's Club. It opened in Reno in the late 1930s and was owned by Harold Smith. Harold's Club was very popular with the large crowds who came to play the card games and slot machines. One popular attraction was a "rodent run," where customers could bet on mice that raced around a small track.

When the United States entered World War I in 1917, the silver and gold deposits of Nevada were almost depleted. To make weapons, the war industries needed copper, zinc, and other metals, which Nevadans mined for a good profit. But after the war ended in 1918, so did the demand, and many mines folded once again.

In 1931, the federal government began a giant public works project, the Hoover Dam. (This was originally called the Boulder Dam.) Built along the Colorado River, it was completed in 1936. At the time it was built, the Hoover Dam project offset Nevada's high unemployment rate. The project provided work to more than five thousand women and men for five years. The dam's wall is higher than a sixty-story skyscraper and is so thick that a two-lane highway could run across its width along the top. More than 7 million tons (6.3 million metric tons) of concrete were used to make the great concrete colossus. Called by newspapers of the time the Eighth Wonder of the World, it changed life in the West for all time by providing electrical power and water for irrigation for parts of California, Arizona, and Nevada.

▲ Once legalized, gambling became a major source of revenue for Nevada. Here, adults have fun gambling in a Reno casino.

Boomtown

For most of its history, the state of Nevada has mandated legalized gambling. During the 1930s, as public works projects and agriculture began to revitalize Nevada's economy, the gaming industry grew. It would eventually become the state's leading industry and change the face of the region, and its reputation, for years to come. Nevada became a destination for tourists seeking entertainment. Visitors also flocked there to take advantage of a law passed in 1931 that made it easy and quick to obtain a divorce.

During World War II, Nevada's mining industry boomed. Military suppliers needed copper, lead, and other metals to build weapons and machinery to support the war effort. In 1950, a historic development took place when the U.S.

DID YOU KNOW?

Slot machines are one of the favorite games that adult visitors play when they visit Nevada's casinos. The first slot machine was invented in 1899 by Charles Fey. Named the Liberty Belle, it became the model for all future slot machines.

government's Atomic Energy Commission chose to make a region northwest of Las Vegas into a nuclear testing site. Nuclear weapons began to be tested there the following year. At the Nevada Test Site, from 1951 to 1962, 126 aboveground tests were carried out; from 1962 to 1992, 925 underground tests were carried out. More than ten thousand people, including many scientists, worked at the site. Yet to be assessed, the environmental damage caused by the blasts has caused great controversy over the years. The commission began to develop peaceful uses for nuclear energy there in 1962.

Recent History

Tourism, manufacturing, and construction have grown to become Nevada's top industries. The gaming industry has diversified to include family entertainment and attractions other than gambling. Major improvements in the state's airports have been under way in order to handle the growing numbers of visitors. The rapid development of Nevada's major cities has spurred the need for better services, such as stronger police and fire departments and better public transportation for its citizens. Air and water pollution, by-products of this quick growth, have become a major focus.

Howard Hughes

The eccentric billionaire Howard Hughes moved to Nevada in 1966. He invested enormous amounts of money in Las Vegas, becoming a major economic force in the city and the state. He bought hotels, casinos, and airports. Hughes was ahead of his time in that he used computers to keep track of inventory supplies for his restaurants and hotels. He also employed surveillance cameras in his casinos to prevent cheating. He is well known for providing excellent benefits and working conditions for his employees in the casinos. Hughes predicted that Las Vegas would continue to grow and flourish; his vision was correct.

Left: Howard Hughes's flying boat, with an eight-story-tall tail section, was nicknamed the "Spruce Goose." Here, it glides over the water in 1947 near Long Beach, California. It flew only once for about a mile (1.6 kilometers).

Individualists

> The country is fabulously rich in gold,
> silver, copper, lead, coal, iron, quicksilver, marble, granite,
> chalk, plaster of Paris (gypsum), thieves,
> murderers, desperadoes, ladies, children, lawyers,
> Christians, Indians, Chinamen, Spaniards, gamblers,
> sharpers, coyotes (pronounced Ki-yo-ties),
> poets, preachers, and jackass rabbits.
>
> — *Mark Twain,* Roughing It *(1872), describing*
> *his experiences in Nevada and California*

In the year 2000, the population of Nevada was 1,998,257, an increase from the 1,201,833 people who lived there in 1990, making it the fastest growing state in the nation. Nevada is not a populous state when compared to many other states, ranking thirty-fifth in population size; nor is it very densely populated. Nevada only has 18.2 people per square mile (7 per sq km). Compare this with Rhode Island, which has 1,003 people per square mile (387 per sq km). Open space still rules in Nevada.

Age Distribution in Nevada
(2000 Census)

0–4	145,817
5–19	415,684
20–24	130,006
25–44	628,572
45–64	459,249
65 & over	218,929

Patterns of Immigration

The total number of people who immigrated to Nevada in 1998 was 6,106. Of that number, the largest immigrant groups were from Mexico (47.2%), the Philippines (11.7%), and China (3.8%).

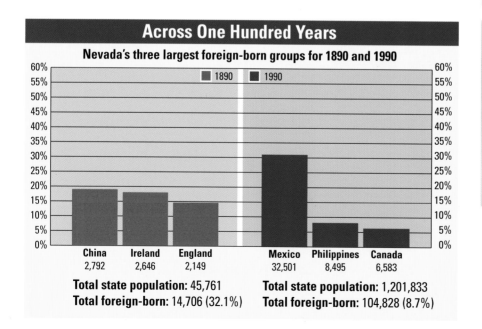

Across One Hundred Years
Nevada's three largest foreign-born groups for 1890 and 1990

■ 1890 ■ 1990

China 2,792	Ireland 2,646	England 2,149	Mexico 32,501	Philippines 8,495	Canada 6,583

Total state population: 45,761
Total foreign-born: 14,706 (32.1%)

Total state population: 1,201,833
Total foreign-born: 104,828 (8.7%)

Many people in the state are employed in urban areas in service businesses that support the tourist and gaming industries. Almost 90 percent of Nevada's population lives in urban locations, but these regions are small. Nevada's largest cities, in order of population size, are Las Vegas, Paradise, Reno, Henderson, and Sunrise Manor. About three-fifths of the state's population lives in or outside of Las Vegas. Reno, located in the western part of Nevada, is another city popular with tourists and is the state's center for commerce, transportation, and banking.

▲ The Fallon All-Indian Rodeo and Powwow features a Native American dance competition.

Ethnicities

About 26,420 Native Americans, descendants of the Shoshone, Paiute, and Washoe who first inhabited Nevada, still reside in the state today. About half live on reservations, such as Pyramid Lake in Washoe County; Western Shoshone, located on the Idaho-Nevada border; and Walker River, which is east of Carson City. The earliest non-Native settlers in Nevada were Hispanic. Las Vegas, discovered by Mexicans in search of a short cut to Los

Heritage and Background, Nevada — Year 2000

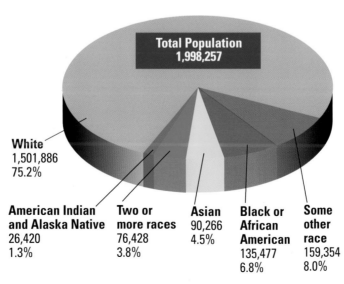

▶ Here is a look at the racial backgrounds of Nevadans today. Nevada ranks twenty-fourth among all U.S. states with regard to African Americans as a percentage of the population.

Total Population 1,998,257

Note: 19.7% (393,970) of the population identify themselves as **Hispanic** or **Latino,** a cultural designation that crosses racial lines. Hispanics and Latinos are counted in this category as well as the racial category of their choice.

White 1,501,886 75.2%

Native Hawaiian and Other Pacific Islander 8,426 0.4%

American Indian and Alaska Native 26,420 1.3%

Two or more races 76,428 3.8%

Asian 90,266 4.5%

Black or African American 135,477 6.8%

Some other race 159,354 8.0%

Angeles, California, supports a large Hispanic community, and the entire state is influenced by their culture.

A few settlers of European descent came to Nevada in the first half of the nineteenth century, but the majority flocked to the state when the Comstock Lode was discovered in 1859. Some settlers came from the eastern part of the United States. Others came from California in the west. At least half, however, were of foreign birth, coming from Germany, Scotland, Wales, England, Canada, and Ireland. Many of these immigrants worked in Nevada's copper mines. Basque settlers from the Pyrenees, the mountains bordering France and Spain, became

Educational Levels of Nevada Workers (age 25 and over)
Less than 9th grade 84,237
9th to 12th grade, no diploma 169,137
High school graduate, including equivalency 384,270
Some college, no degree or associate degree 434,657
Bachelor's degree 158,078
Graduate or professional degree 79,797

▼ Hotels light up the skyline of Las Vegas, Nevada's largest city.

sheepherders in Nevada. Portuguese and Italian immigrants became farmers. By 1920, the number of newcomers declined. Then, after World War II, the population of Nevada began to grow again, as Californians and others moved to the area.

Today, about 90 percent of Nevadans are of European or Mexican heritage. About 7 percent are African Americans. The others are Native Americans, Asians, and Pacific Islanders.

Religion

The largest religious groups in Nevada today are Roman Catholics, Mormons, and Protestants. Roman Catholics number about 159,000 and Mormons, about 89,000. Protestants, including Episcopalians, Baptists, and Methodists, number about 90,000. There are also about 20,000 Jews in Nevada today.

Education

Before 1861, when Nevada became a territory, the educational system was very haphazard. Schools were built and teachers assembled in one area, but as new mining discoveries were made elsewhere, families rushed to the new region. Schools and teachers often followed.

After 1861, laws were made to provide public education funded by county taxes. When Nevada acquired statehood, school districts were established. Today, there are seventeen county districts. There are approximately 470 elementary and secondary schools in the state, and almost ten thousand children attend private school.

In 1864, the University of Nevada was founded by the state constitution. It was established in Elko in 1874 and moved to Reno in 1886. The Mackay School of Mines in Reno is renowned for its engineering and mining disciplines. Today's university system includes schools in Reno and Las Vegas, as well as community colleges in Elko, Sparks, North Las Vegas, and Carson City.

▲ The Fourth Ward School was built in 1876 during the height of the mining boom in Virginia City. This former public school is now a museum.

Powwows

A powwow is a gathering of Native American people. It is often highlighted by dance ceremonies, with different peoples adding their own variations. Visitors are encouraged to attend.

Deserts, Mountains, and Canyons

> Home means Nevada
> Home means the hills,
> Home means the sage and the pine.
> Out by the Truckee, silvery rills,
> Out where the sun always shines,
> Here is the land which I love the best,
> Fairer than all I can see.
> Deep in the heart of the golden west
> Home means Nevada to me.
> — *"Home Means Nevada," state song*
> *by Bertha Raffetto, adopted February 6, 1933*

Nevada is a western mountain state that lies almost entirely in a large desert area called the Great Basin. It is bordered in the west and southwest by California and on the north by Oregon and Idaho. The Colorado River and Arizona form the southeastern border. To the east is Utah.

Nevada is the driest state in the nation, because the mountain area known as the Sierra Nevada, in the western part of the state, rises high, cutting off rain-bearing wind and clouds from the Pacific Ocean.

Nevada has three main geographical regions: the Sierra Nevada, the Columbia Plateau, and the Basin and Range Region.

Highest Point
Boundary Peak
13,140 feet (4,005 m)
above sea level

▼ *From left to right*: Lake Tahoe in summer; rock arch, Valley of Fire State Park; Hoover Dam; Dunes in the Big Smoky Valley; Red Rock Canyon; geysers erupt in the Black Rock Desert.

The Sierra Nevada

The rugged mountain range of the Sierra Nevada runs across a small corner of the state to the south and west of Carson City. In the same region are the steep mountains of the Carson Range, extending from California into Nevada. Many hot springs lie at their bases. Beautiful Lake Tahoe, along the California-Nevada border, and many other mountain lakes are also found here.

The Columbia Plateau

The Columbia Plateau lies along the northeastern border of Nevada and Idaho. This vast tableland extends into Oregon and Idaho. A deep bedrock of lava sheets lies underneath. Streams and rivers have cut deep canyons through the bedrock, leaving sharp ridges in many places. These rock cliffs and valleys eventually open up into flat or rolling prairies by the Idaho border.

The Basin and Range Region

The Basin and Range Region makes up the majority of land in the state of Nevada. It is largely an upland region surrounded by approximately 150 mountain ranges. Most of the ranges run north-south across the region. The towering peaks of the Sierra Nevada are at the western edge of the basin area. The Toquima and Toiyabe mountain ranges are located in the middle. The Toana and Snake ranges are to the east. Lone hills called *buttes* and tablelike mountains called *mesas* are found between the mountain ranges. Flat valleys and lakes are also located between the mountains. There is great variation between the lowest and highest points in the Basin and Range Region. The highest point is Boundary Peak — 13,140 feet (4,005 m) high — in the White Mountains in Esmeralda County near California. The lowest area, near the Colorado River, is less than 500

Average January temperature
Elko: 26°F (-5°C)
Las Vegas: 47°F (6°C)

Average July temperature
Elko: 69°F (21°C)
Las Vegas: 91°F (32°C)

Average yearly rainfall
Elko: 9 inches (23 cm)
Las Vegas: 4 inches (10 cm)

Average yearly snowfall
Elko: 40 inches (102 cm)
Las Vegas: 1 inch (2.5 cm)

DID YOU KNOW?

The boundary between Nevada and California runs at a sharp angle west to east, placing Nevada's capital, Carson City, farther west than the city of Los Angeles.

Largest Lakes

Lake Mead
157,400 acres (63,902 ha)

Pyramid Lake
117,400 acres (47,512 hectares)

Lake Tahoe
122,000 acres (49,454 ha)

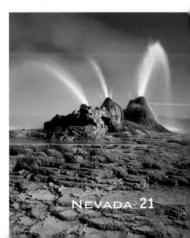

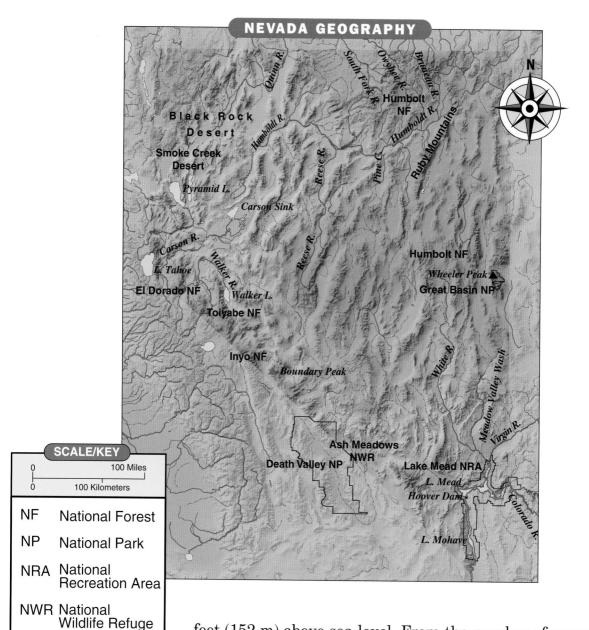

SCALE/KEY

0   100 Miles

0   100 Kilometers

NF	National Forest
NP	National Park
NRA	National Recreation Area
NWR	National Wildlife Refuge
▲	Highest Point
▲	Important Peaks
▨	Mountains

feet (152 m) above sea level. From the number of geysers
and hot springs in the region, geologists can conclude that
Nevada was once a largely volcanic area.

Rivers and Lakes

Nevada's rivers flow only during the wet season, which
lasts from December to June. Most empty into the Great
Basin, running into lakes that have no outlets or into low,
shallow spots in the earth called *sinks*. Lake Tahoe is
known as one of the loveliest mountain lakes in the nation.
Pyramid Lake is a remnant of an ancient lake that dried
up. Lake Mead was created when the Hoover Dam was
built across the Colorado River. It is the only lake in

Nevada with an outlet to the sea and measures nearly 157,900 acres (63,902 ha).

Plants and Animals

Many of the mountainsides in Nevada are forested with willow, spruce, hemlock, fir, cottonwood, alder, pine, and juniper trees. Sagebrush, mesquite, rabbitbrush, and bitterbrush are also commonly seen. Cacti and yucca plants are at home in the Nevada desert. After snows melt in spring, the desert blooms with colorful wildflowers. In the mountain and valley meadows, grasses thrive and meadows bloom with shooting stars, violets, Indian paintbrush, and larkspur.

Nevada's wildlife includes foxes, marmots, coyotes, and mink. Reptiles such as snakes and lizards live in the desert. In Pyramid Lake, hundreds of white pelicans make their nests at the Anaho Island Refuge. The endangered cui-ui fish is found only in Pyramid Lake. Nevada is also famous for its Lahontan cutthroat trout and the Devil's Hole pupfish, found nowhere else in the world but Devil's Hole. Elusive desert bighorn sheep scavenge the mountain ranges looking for food in an environment relatively barren of vegetation.

Major Rivers

Colorado River
1,450 miles (2,333 km)

Humboldt River
300 miles (483 km)

Carson River
125 miles (201 km)

▼ The desert tortoise has lived in the arid southwestern United States for the last ten thousand to twelve thousand years. The tortoise is now threatened by human population pressures.

Games, Services, and Ranches

> It's not hard. It's not grueling to me to get up in the morning and go out. But there's always one thing — if you get tired and whatever, you can lay down and go to sleep anyplace because you're the boss. I enjoy this type of work. It's not the same thing day in and day out.
>
> — *Rancher Ted Zimmerman,*
> *quoted in* Nevada *by Kathleen Thompson*

A state's gross state product is the total value of all goods and services produced in the state in a year. In Nevada, the biggest portion of the gross state product is provided by service industries. Establishments such as restaurants, casinos, hotels, and ski resorts provide services to the vast number of tourists who visit. Wholesale and retail trade makes up another important part of the state's economy. Manufacturing, construction, and agriculture are major industries, but they are not as important in Nevada as they are in many other states. Mining, mostly of gold and nonmetallic minerals, remains an important industry.

Nevada's natural resources — its mineral deposits and varied landscape — have given rise to industries best able to utilize them. Mining led to an increase in the state's population, which, in turn, brought ranchers who realized that the thick grasses of Nevada's valleys were ideal for grazing cattle.

Agriculture and Mining

Ranches and farms occupy about one-eighth of Nevada, and livestock ranching is the major agricultural industry. There are about three thousand ranches and farms in the state. The cattle graze for part of the year on grassland owned by the federal government, which the ranch owners rent.

Hay for livestock feed is Nevada's most important crop. It is harvested in the northwest basins of the state. Other crops

Top Employers
(of workers age sixteen and over)

Services	51.9%
Wholesale and retail trade	14.0%
Construction	9.2%
Transportation, communications, and public utilities	7.4%
Finance, insurance, and real estate	6.5%
Manufacturing	4.9%
Federal, state, and local government (including military)	4.5%
Agriculture, forestry, fisheries, and mining	1.6%

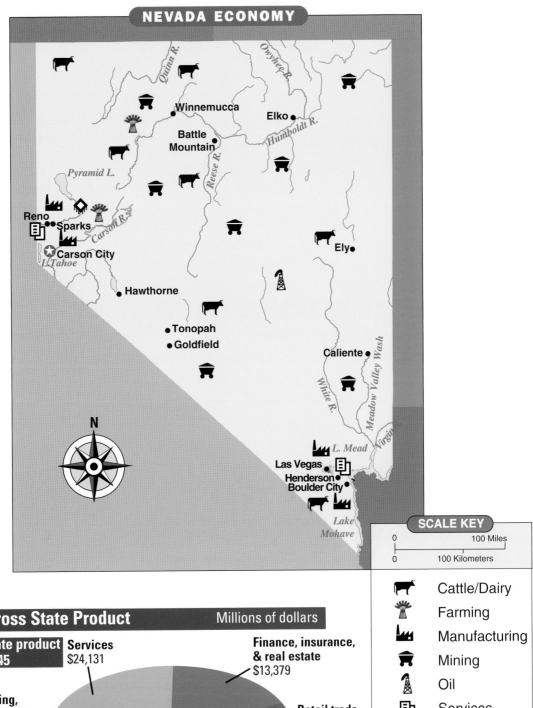

NEVADA ECONOMY

SCALE KEY

0 — 100 Miles
0 — 100 Kilometers

- Cattle/Dairy
- Farming
- Manufacturing
- Mining
- Oil
- Services
- Technology

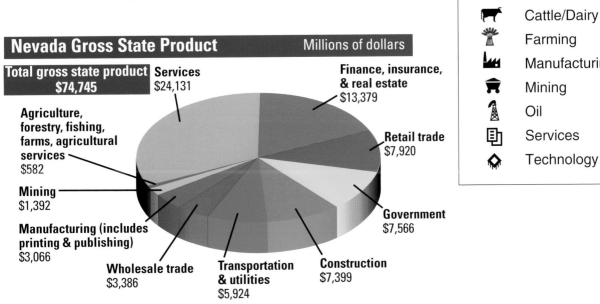

Nevada Gross State Product

Millions of dollars

Total gross state product $74,745

- Services $24,131
- Finance, insurance, & real estate $13,379
- Retail trade $7,920
- Agriculture, forestry, fishing, farms, agricultural services $582
- Mining $1,392
- Manufacturing (includes printing & publishing) $3,066
- Wholesale trade $3,386
- Transportation & utilities $5,924
- Construction $7,399
- Government $7,566

include alfalfa seed, onions, barley, wheat, garlic, and potatoes. In the north, west, and southeast, farms are irrigated near river valleys. In the rest of the state, water is pumped from wells to irrigate farmlands.

Mining is an important part of Nevada's economy, and the state leads the nation in the production of gold. Nevada produces two-thirds of all the gold mined in the United States. Nevada is also the nation's leading producer of silver ore.

Other important minerals mined in Nevada include petroleum and diatomite, which is a chalky substance. Barite, limestone, salt, gravel and sand, clay, gypsum, and magnesite are also mined, as well as gemstones such as fire opals and turquoise.

Manufacturing

Nevada's tax structure is appealing to both business owners and employees alike. There are no corporate or personal income taxes in the state, encouraging the growth of all kinds of industry.

The main manufacturing industries in Nevada were once the processing of mineral products and the production of agricultural goods. Today that has changed, and the leading manufactured items are printed materials, machinery, food products, and concrete.

Carson City, Reno, and Las Vegas are major manufacturing centers for the state. Chemical-processing plants are found in Henderson, which is near the Hoover Dam and uses power from the dam to run its factories.

Warehousing, Services, and Tourism

Warehousing is an important service industry in Nevada. The state has a free-port law, which means that products can be stored tax-free if they will be sent to locations outside of the state for sale later. Reno and Las Vegas have many warehouses where goods are stored.

▲ The bright lights of Las Vegas shine twenty-four hours a day as tourists flock to the city for entertainment and gambling.

Powerfully Hot!

It is hot beneath much of Nevada. The heat comes from numerous geothermal sources below Earth's surface. Scientists have found that more than 10 million acres (4 million ha) of Nevada have the potential to be developed as a source of geothermal energy. If established, this new industry would provide a clean alternative source of power. The new power source would support a big industry in itself, plus it would provide the energy to power other sectors of Nevada's economy, stimulating further economic growth.

Service industries provide the biggest number of jobs for Nevadans and, as a whole, are much more important to Nevada's economy than in many other states. Las Vegas and Reno form the two major hubs for service industries, and much of the revenue comes from the tourist trade. Billions of dollars are contributed to Nevada's economy each year by the more than forty million visitors who enjoy the state's gaming, entertainment, and scenic beauty. Leading service industries include finance, insurance, and real estate. There are also hotels, hospitals, data processing, and retail establishments, all catering to the year-round influx of tourists. In fact, the state's taxes on services catering to the tourism industry supply more than 50 percent of its annual revenue. The government is also an important part of the service economy, employing thousands at important federal facilities, including Nellis Air Force Base, just north of Las Vegas, and the U.S. Department of Energy's Nevada Test Site.

▲ At the Indepedence Gold Mine in the Humboldt National Forest, earth-moving equipment cuts into the hills.

Transportation

Nevada has approximately 46,000 miles (74,001 km) of highways and roads, and the state road system is considered excellent. Federal highways cross the state from both north and south and from east and west. There are four rail lines, which are used for moving freight. Passenger trains are found in several cities. The state has two major airports, McCarran International in Las Vegas and Reno/Tahoe International in Reno, plus approximately 52 small, local airports and 25 heliports. The international airports are among the busiest in the world, but the smaller facilities handle traffic to the more remote areas of the state.

Made in Nevada

Leading farm products and crops
Beef cattle
Milk
Alfalfa seed
Hay
Potatoes
Sheep

Other products
Printed materials
Food products
Glass, stone, and clay products
Electronic equipment
Plastics
Chemicals
Aerospace
Metal products
Machinery
Gold
Silver
Nonmetallic minerals
Sand and gravel
Petroleum
Stone

Major Airports		
Airport	Location	Passengers per year (2000)
McCarran International	Las Vegas	36,865,866
Reno/Tahoe International	Reno	5,624,535

Leader Among States

> All political power is inherent in the people. Government is instituted for the protection, security and benefit of the people; and they have the right to alter or reform the same whenever the public good may require it.
>
> — *Nevada Constitution, Article I, Section 2 (as amended 1974)*

Nevada's state constitution was adopted in 1864, the year that the state entered the Union. Today, Nevada is still governed under the original constitution and the amendments that have been passed since that time. For an amendment, or change, to be accepted, it must have the approval of a majority of the voters. To vote in Nevada one must be a resident of the state for at least thirty days and must be eighteen years old.

The system of government in Nevada is like that of the U.S. federal government. It is divided into three branches: executive, legislative, and judicial. The executive branch administers laws, the legislative branch makes laws, and the judicial branch interprets laws.

The state of Nevada is represented in the federal government by two senators in the U.S. Senate. In the U.S. House of Representatives, Nevada has two representatives. Nevada has four electoral votes in presidential elections. Since its earliest days, Nevada's legislature has led the country in adopting new laws in the areas of voting rights for women, the public's right to referendums and ballot initiatives, and many other progressive ideas.

The Executive Branch

Nevada's chief executive officer is the governor, who is elected every four years to a limit of two terms. The governor's job is to make sure the laws of the state are carried out. Serving as the state's chief law enforcement

State Constitution

"We the people of the State of Nevada, Grateful to Almighty God for our freedom in order to secure its blessings, insure domestic tranquillity, and form a more perfect Government, do establish this Constitution."

— *Preamble to the amended Nevada State Constitution*

Elected Posts in the Executive Branch		
Office	Length of Term	Term Limits
Governor	4 years	2 terms
Lieutenant Governor	4 years	2 terms
Secretary of State	4 years	2 terms
Treasurer	4 years	2 terms
Controller	4 years	2 terms
Attorney General	4 years	2 terms

official, the governor has the power to call out the National Guard in an emergency.

Other elected state officials are the lieutenant governor, secretary of state, treasurer, controller, and attorney general, whose terms are also four years. There are approximately 150 officials of the executive branch belonging to commissions and administrative boards. The governor appoints these people.

The Legislative Branch

The legislative branch, which makes Nevada's laws, is made up of two bodies, the senate and the assembly. The legislature meets in regular sessions on the first Monday of February in odd-numbered years. Regular sessions may last 120 days. Special sessions may be called by the governor. The Senate has twenty-one members, and the Assembly has forty-two members, each representing a district. Senators serve four-year terms and cannot be elected more than three times. Assembly members serve two-year terms and serve no more than six

▼ With its famous six-sided silver dome and native sandstone walls, the capitol in Carson City is the second oldest capitol west of the Mississippi River.

terms. Legislators have the job of discussing and debating new laws, which are called bills. Before a bill becomes a law, it must be approved by both houses of the legislature. Then it goes to the governor for signing. After it has the governor's signature, the bill becomes law. If the governor vetoes, or refuses to sign a bill, it goes back to the legislature. If both houses reapprove the proposed law by a two-thirds vote, the bill becomes a law despite the governor's veto.

The Judicial Branch

The job of the judicial branch is to interpret Nevada's laws. The high court of the judicial branch of the state government is the Nevada Supreme Court. Below it are district courts and municipal and justice courts. The supreme court is composed of a chief justice and six associate justices. They are elected to six-year terms. One or two justices are elected to the court every two years. The most senior justice serves as the chief justice. If the supreme court rules that a new law violates the intent of the Nevada constitution, then the law can be rejected. There are nine district courts in Nevada, and those districts that have large populations are divided into departments. Each department has a district judge as its head. City courts have municipal judges. Townships have justices of the peace. All judges in the state serve no more than two terms.

Local Government

There are sixteen counties and one independent city (Carson City) in Nevada, and they are governed by elected boards of county commissioners made up of three members, serving four-year terms. Other officials in the counties who are elected by the voters are the assessor, auditor and recorder, sheriff, clerk, public administrator, and district attorney. Local government officials serve for no more than twelve years. The majority of cities in Nevada have a

Legislature			
House	Number of Members	Length of Term	Term Limits
Senate	21 senators	4 years	3 terms
Assembly	42 assemblymen	2 years	6 terms

mayor-council form of government. Important services are provided by the local governments, including the funding of school systems, police forces, and road maintenance.

Nevada Politics

There are more registered Democrats than Republicans in Nevada. About half of the voters in the state live in Clark County, where the Democratic party maintains a stronghold. Voters in Nevada have elected more Democratic governors than Republican; however, Nevada has voted for more Republican presidential candidates than Democratic. The diverse population of Nevada is well represented by the ethnic differences among the state's elected officials and leaders.

The Federal Government and Nevada

The federal government owns about 85 percent of the land in Nevada. Only Alaska has more federally owned land. As the largest property holder in Nevada, the federal government has a lot of power over the state's economy and policies. There is an ongoing dispute between the federal government and many Nevadans about the use of Yucca Mountain. The federal government plans to use the site to dispose of nuclear waste. Many citizens of the state are adamantly opposed to the plan because they feel it will harm the environment.

The vast areas of land owned by the federal government are overseen by federal agencies, such as the Fish and Wildlife Service, the Forest Service, the Bureau of Land Management, and the National Park Service. These agencies are active in ensuring the survival of Nevada's wildlife and natural beauty. The land management agency is also instrumental in negotiating between businesses that want to use land for development and citizens concerned with environmental issues and explosive growth.

Where the Money Comes From

Most revenue, or income, to run the state comes from taxes. A sales tax on various items is the most important source of income. The second most important tax is on many kinds of gambling. Nevada permits many forms of gambling that are not legal in other states. This brings gamblers to the state and generates income via taxes. There are no personal or corporate taxes in Nevada. State and local governments are paid for by property taxes.

▼ Nevada state Senate in session. The Nevada Legislature meets once every two years for 120 days. The governor may call a special session if the need arises.

History, Culture, and Fun

In the atom's fizz and pop we heard possibility
uncorked . . . The world was beginning
all over again, fresh and hot;
we could have anything we wanted.

— *Lynn Emanuel, from "The Planet Krypton,"*
a poem on watching atomic bomb testing
in Nevada, 1992

Both visitors and residents enjoy Nevada's dramatic desertscapes, forests, lakes, and snow-covered mountains. Historical sites, national parks, mining ghost towns of the Old West, and museums of all kinds abound in Nevada. Las Vegas is home to world-famous hotels, restaurants, and casinos, and the city plays host to many renowned entertainers.

National and state recreational areas attract many visitors to Nevada. About 7 percent of the state is covered by national forests. Among these are Humboldt-Toiyabe National Forest in central and western Nevada, Humboldt National Forest in the northeastern part of the state, and small parts of the Eldorado and Inyo National Forests, which Nevada shares with California. Nevada also shares Death Valley

DID YOU KNOW?

The small settlement that grew to be the big city of Reno was named in 1868 by one of the builders of the Central Pacific Railroad. The city is named in honor of General Jesse Lee Reno of West Virginia, who was killed in a Civil War battle in 1862.

◄ A pack llama leads a hiker along the scenic Ruby Crest Trail in the Ruby Mountains. The range was named in the 1880s during the days of the gold rush. Gold panners found garnets which they confused with rubies.

National Park with California. Colorful mountains, desert plants, and a deep valley are found there. The Lake Mead National Recreation Area, which is shared by Nevada and Arizona, is run by the National Park Service. The area contains the huge Hoover Dam (formerly the Boulder Dam). Visitors travel by elevator deep to the base of the dam to view the inner workings of the power plant. Lake Mead, an enormous lake created when the dam was built, is a recreation area for camping, swimming, fishing, sailing, and waterskiing. The Lehman Caves near Wheeler Peak in eastern Nevada have tall limestone columns and shield-shaped rock formations.

Among the many state parks and monuments are Valley of Fire State Park, which contains red sandstone cliffs and rocks with carvings made by prehistoric peoples, and Cathedral Gorge State Park, north of Caliente, which has towering cliffs carved into fantastic shapes by water and wind. Hot springs and geysers are also found in Nevada. They include Steamboat Springs, south of Reno; Gerlach, in northwest Nevada; and Diana's Punch Bowl, in northern Nye County. Ash Meadows National Wildlife Refuge features wetland areas with springs, small reservoirs, and Devil's Hole cave, just nine miles from Death Valley Junction at the edge of the Mojave Desert.

Nevada's Cowboys

Large cattle ranches still operate in northern Nevada, which is known by residents as "Cowboy Country." The Buckaroo Hall of Fame, in the town of Winnemucca, commemorates the cowboys who worked on the state's cattle ranches in the 1880s. *Buckaroo* is a word that means "cowboy." Nearby is the Spur Cross Dude Ranch, where visitors can actively take part in the cowboy way of life. People who stay at the dude ranch help real ranchers carry out their daily tasks.

Old mining towns and ghost towns are found throughout Nevada, allowing visitors to explore this chapter of the country's past. Virginia City, north of Carson City, is the most famous, but others are found in Austin, Eureka, Goldfield, and Tonopah.

Libraries and Museums

Nevada's large towns and cities have public libraries. In total, there are about eighty public libraries in the state. Carson City is the home of the Nevada State Library and Archives. This huge collection of government documents and books numbers over three hundred thousand publications, including a highly valuable collection of law books and records. The Nevada Historical Society, located in Reno, houses important historical records.

The Nevada State Museum in Carson City has a collection of historical relics and examples of Nevada wildlife. Life-sized exhibits built in tunnels below the building show authentic mining operations, such as drilling, blasting, and hoisting. The museum, once the site

▲ The Nevada State Museum and Historical Society in Las Vegas seeks to preserve Nevada's past for present and future generations. Its exhibits promote an understanding of the prehistory, history and natural history of the state.

of the U.S. Mint in Carson City, houses an impressive coin collection. The museum also houses exhibits about Nevada's history and the lives of prehistoric and contemporary Native American peoples.

The Nevada Historical Society Museums in Reno and Las Vegas also have varied exhibits, including furnishings and clothing used by pioneers of Nevada, Native American baskets, paintings, cattle brands, musical instruments, embroidery, and china.

The Nevada Museum of Art in Reno was founded in 1931 and is the oldest cultural organization in the state. Its collections, including painting and sculpture, focus on themes of the land and the environment. In addition to its exhibit space, the museum also offers fine arts classes for children and adults.

In Reno, the Mackay School of Mines Museum has exhibits on geology, the study of metals, and the history of mining in Nevada. The Lost City Museum of Archaeology, located in Overton, displays items excavated at the site of an ancient Native American settlement called the Pueblo

▼ Historic towns offer authentic re-enactments of early life in Nevada, featuring costumed actors.

Grande de Nevada. The Old Las Vegas Mormon Fort in Las Vegas exhibits historical relics of the Mormon pioneers.

Nevada's first zoo, Southern Nevada Zoological-Botanical Park, was opened in 1980 and houses more than two hundred animals. It is the only place in the United States where one can view the Barbary ape from North Africa. Nevada's largest zoo, Sierra Safari Zoo, opened in 1990 and is just north of Reno. It houses only animals bred in captivity. There are wildlife and conservation parks throughout the state, in addition to animal attractions featuring dolphins, exotic tigers, and extraordinary horses.

▲ Basque culture, common to the Pyrenees Mountains between France and Spain, is as prevalent in Elko as the cowboy lifestyle. Pictured are Basques in native costume at an Elko festival.

Communications

Newspapers have always been important to Nevadans. The first ones were handwritten news sheets. The *Territorial Enterprise,* published originally in Genoa in 1858, was the first printed newspaper in the state. When the mining population moved, the paper moved, too. Its new home was Virginia City, where the famous American author Mark Twain worked as a young reporter during the 1860s. There are seven daily newspapers published in the state today. Those with the biggest circulation are the *Las Vegas Sun*, the *Las Vegas Review-Journal*, and the *Reno Gazette Journal*. There are twelve television stations in the state, seven cable television systems, and about thirty radio stations. The first radio station started broadcasting from Reno in 1928. The first television stations began broadcasting from Reno and Las Vegas in 1953.

Sports

Although Nevada has no major league sports teams, its citizens are avid fans of college basketball and football at the University of Nevada, at Las Vegas and Reno. The men's basketball team at UNLV, the Running Rebels, consistently draws thousands of people to its games.

More than one hundred golf courses are found in Nevada, with most in Reno and Las Vegas. In October each year, Las Vegas hosts the Las Vegas Invitational Golf Tournament. This famous event draws top golfers from around the world. The sport of boxing brought great attention to Reno when, in 1910, the city hosted a match between a black heavyweight and a white challenger. The reputation of Nevada as an upstart state was confirmed when the city of Reno came forward and offered to build a stadium for the match, just as officials in San Francisco, California, were bowing out of hosting the event due to antiboxing pressure. Today, Nevada remains a popular choice of location for professional boxing matches.

Rodeo competitions are also common in Nevada. Winnemucca is popular for its U.S. Team Roping Championship. Three thousand teams of cowboys come from throughout the West to compete and win prizes. Downhill skiing is very popular in the mountainous regions of the state. Squaw Valley, near Reno, hosted the 1960 Winter Olympic Games. Skiing is also popular at Lake Tahoe and in the Ruby Mountains, in the eastern part of the state. Cross-country skiers are challenged by Nevada's spectacular terrain. The rugged mountains, lakes, and forests of Nevada are ideal for hiking, mountain biking, and fishing.

Nevada Greats

Jerry Tarkanian is Nevada's best-known and best-loved basketball coach. He served as coach for the Running Rebels for nineteen seasons at the University of Nevada at Las Vegas. During that time, the team won 83 percent of its games. That is the highest percentage of wins for any college basketball coach. Tarkanian's coaching career spanned thirty-six years, ending with his retirement in 1992.

Andre Agassi was born in Las Vegas on April 29, 1970. When Agassi was eighteen, he was the youngest American tennis player to achieve the number one ranking. This famous athlete has won many tennis tournaments, including Wimbledon in 1992, the U.S. Open in 1994 and 1999, and the Australian Open in 1995, 2000, and 2001. Agassi's foundation provides recreational and educational opportunities for at-risk girls and boys.

▶ A group of children from the West Las Vegas Arts Center with tennis star Andre Agassi during rehearsals for the Andre Agassi Charitable Foundation's concert on October 4, 1997. The concert benefited the Andre Agassi Charitable Foundation, which was founded in 1994 to help at-risk Las Vegas children.

Noteworthy Nevadans

> My feeling is that landscape is character, not background.
> It's not a stage. It's an active agent. It must be.
> — *Author Walter Van Tilburg Clark,*
> *describing his Nevada roots*
> *in an interview in 1932*

Following are only a few of the thousands of people who were born, died, or spent much of their lives in Nevada and made extraordinary contributions to the state and the nation.

JOHN WILLIAM MACKAY
FINANCIER

BORN: *November 28, 1831, Dublin, Ireland*
DIED: *July 20, 1902, London, England*

A noted philanthropist and visionary, John William Mackay is the most renowned of the Comstock Mine owners. In 1840, at the age of nine, he arrived in New York with his parents and immediately went to work in a shipyard. Mackay answered the call to "go west" in 1850. After making and losing money at mining gold in California, he went to Virginia City and established the business that would discover the great Bonanza vein of the Comstock Lode, which, by 1877, was making tens of millions of dollars. Seeing communications as the future of the rapidly growing nation, Mackay started the Commercial Cable Company in 1884 to compete with other telegraph companies of the day. He initiated and completed the production of two transatlantic cables and is responsible for driving the price of transatlantic messages down. The Mackay School of Mines at the University of Nevada was founded by Mackay's widow and son in 1908.

MARK TWAIN
AUTHOR

BORN: *November 30, 1835, Florida, MO*
DIED: *April 21, 1910, Redding, CT*

Mark Twain, born Samuel Longhorne Clemens, was a master of humor, pathos, and sarcasm and is one of the most influential modern American writers. *The Adventures of Huckleberry Finn* (1885) is considered by many to be the first modern American novel. Mark Twain's career as a river pilot was cut short by the Civil War. He came to Nevada as a young man in his twenties, hoping to get rich quickly by investing in mining operations. He soon met with failure and instead became a reporter in Virginia City for the *Territorial Enterprise*. As a columnist, Twain honed his writing skills in preparation for many great novels including *The Adventures of Tom Sawyer* (1876) and *The Prince and the Pauper* (1882). *Roughing It* (1872) is his memoir of his years in the U.S. western frontier. He is a familiar image today, wearing his famous white suit, and his intelligent, outrageous observations are frequently quoted.

SARAH WINNEMUCCA
NATIVE AMERICAN ADVOCATE

BORN: *1844, Lovelock*
DIED: *October 17, 1891, Monida, MT*

Sarah Winnemucca was the daughter and granddaughter of chiefs of the Paiute, a people known for their friendship and cooperation with white settlers. As a young girl, she made a visit to California, where she developed an interest in white people and their culture. She became one of only two members of her people to learn English, and she used her language skills to mediate between her Native people and the white settlers. The U.S. Army hired Winnemucca to serve as an interpreter between the U.S. government and several Native groups it was battling. When the Paiute joined with the Bannock of Idaho to fight against settlers encroaching upon their land, she traveled to Idaho to convince her father to end the bloodshed and return home to Nevada.

Winnemucca witnessed firsthand the cruel treatment of her people at the hands of white political leaders, and she spent her life fighting for the Native Americans through traditional channels of white government. She testified before Congress and lectured throughout the East about the unfair, violent treatment of Native Americans throughout the West. When she returned to Nevada, she opened a school for Native children and wrote her autobiography, *Life Among the Paiutes: Their Wrongs and Claims*. She is remembered as "The Princess" by white people and "Mother" by the Paiutes. The city of Winnemucca is named for her great family.

WOVOKA
NATIVE AMERICAN MYSTIC

BORN: *c. 1856, Esmeralda County*
DIED: *September or October c. 1932, Walker Lake*

Wovoka, a Paiute, was born in western Nevada and became an orphan at the age of fourteen. A white rancher named David Wilson took him in, taught him English, and employed him as a ranch hand into adulthood. Wovoka became known throughout the region as Jack Wilson. Sometime in the late 1880s, he was inspired by the teachings of a Paiute religious mystic named Tavibo. Combining Tavibo's teachings with the Christian culture in which he was raised, Wovoka started a movement called the Ghost Dance religion. His popular message prophesied that if Native

Americans behaved in a righteous and moral way, they would achieve their desire of living in a world free of white oppression and full of great material and spiritual wealth. His followers engaged in ritual dancing which, when performed today, symbolizes a desire to preserve traditional ways. The slaughter of hundreds of Native Americans at Wounded Knee Creek in South Dakota in 1890 forced many of Wovoka's followers to abandon the Ghost Dance religion and give up their dreams of a world free of cruelty at the hands of the whites. Wovoka lived out the rest of his life as Jack Wilson, dying in 1932. Remnants of the Ghost Dance religion can be found in many spiritual elements of the Native cultures surviving today.

KEY PITTMAN
SENATOR

BORN: *September 19, 1872, Vicksburg, MS*
DIED: *November 10, 1940, Reno*

U.S. Senator Key Pittman is more famous for the myth surrounding his death than for his years spent in office. Legend has it that Pittman, a Democrat, up for reelection in 1940 and campaigning in Reno, ended up drinking too much and died of a heart attack before election day. The story goes that his friends kept his body on ice in a hotel bathtub, and his death a secret, to ensure that he would be reelected and his senate seat would remain Democratic. Area newspapers reported that he died on November 10, 1940, only five days after winning the election. In life, Pittman was just as outrageous, having been elected in 1913 by the narrowest margin in the nation at the time. His election was also mysteriously (and illegally) confirmed by the legislature even though Pittman took office by a popular vote at a time when the Nevada state constitution still required legislatures to elect senators.

PATRICK MCCARRAN
ATTORNEY AND JUDGE

BORN: *August 8, 1876, Reno*
DIED: *September 28, 1954, Hawthorne*

Patrick Anthony McCarran was a politician who championed the cause of working people. He was responsible for the nation's first law limiting the workday to eight hours. McCarran worked as a sheepherder while he studied law at the University of Nevada. He was elected to the Nevada legislature in 1903 and served as a district attorney in Nye County and later on the supreme court of Nevada from 1913 to 1918. McCarran served as U.S. senator from 1933 until his death in 1954. He was extremely defense-minded and sponsored many laws intended to improve U.S. security. The McCarran-Woods Act of 1950 excluded registered communists from serving in the government, and the McCarran-Walter Act of 1952 made immigration laws more restrictive. McCarran, however, was an opponent of Senator Joseph McCarthy and his movement to blacklist suspected communists in the 1950s. There is a bronze statue of McCarran in the National Statuary Hall Collection in Washington, D.C.

WALTER VAN TILBURG CLARK
AUTHOR

BORN: *August 3, 1909, East Orland, ME*
DIED: *November 10, 1971, Reno*

Walter Van Tilburg Clark moved to Reno when he was eight years old and was educated at the University of Nevada in Reno. This famous writer of novels and short stories often wrote about the Old West, using familiar Western subjects, such as cowboys and the frontier, to explore larger moral and philosophical issues. His most famous novel, *The Ox-Bow Incident* (1940), is set in Nevada and turned Clark into a critically acclaimed and celebrated author at age thirty. He became writer-in-residence at the University of Nevada in 1962, teaching there until his death.

FRANK SINATRA
ENTERTAINER

BORN: *December 12, 1915, Hoboken, NJ*
DIED: *May 14, 1998, Los Angeles, CA*

A legendary singer and actor, Francis Albert Sinatra dropped out of high school at the age of fifteen to pursue a career in entertainment. He released his first hit song, "All or Nothing at All," in 1943 and became what many consider the country's first superstar. In the 1940s, he became a film sensation, acting in many successful movies and winning an Academy Award in 1953 for Best Supporting Actor in the film *From Here to Eternity*. Sinatra spent much of his career living and performing in Las

Vegas, where he drew crowds in great numbers. His home, "Cal-Neva," on Lake Tahoe's Crystal Bay, straddled the border between Nevada and California. Sinatra and his friends, all entertainers and

members of the fabulous "Rat Pack," ruled the social scene from Las Vegas to Hollywood. In 1997, Sinatra received the Congressional Gold Medal for his many accomplishments as singer, actor, and humanitarian.

GREG LEMOND
PROFESSIONAL CYCLIST

BORN: *June 26, 1961, Median, MN*

Gregory James LeMond is a three-time winner of the Tour de France, the world's most competitive and grueling bike race. LeMond moved to the Washoe Valley at age seven, and at fourteen began cycling competitively in the hills around his home in Reno. He turned pro when he was nineteen and, in 1983, became the first American to win the professional road race at the World Championships, the most prestigious one-day event in the sport. In 1986, at the age of twenty-five, LeMond became the first American ever to win the Tour de France. His career was considered over, however, when he was sidelined in a serious hunting accident in 1987. With thirty shotgun pellets remaining in his body, eight weeks after his near death, LeMond began to train for a comeback. With the help of high-tech equipment and creative racing strategies, he came back to win the Tour de France in 1989 and 1990. He retired in 1994 and continues to cycle and design increasingly sophisticated equipment for the sport.

Nevada
History At-A-Glance

1776
Francisco Garcés is possibly the first non-Native American to travel through present-day Nevada.

1843-45
John C. Frémont and Kit Carson explore and map large regions of Nevada.

1849
Mormon leader Brigham Young creates the State of Deseret, which includes present-day Nevada.

1859
Discovery of silver deposits at the Comstock Lode brings prospectors to western Nevada in a mining boom.

1864
Nevada becomes thirty-sixth state on October 31.

1874
University of Nevada is established at Elko; in 1886, it moves to Reno.

1820-30
Peter Skene Ogden sees Humboldt River; Jedediah S. Smith crosses southern Nevada.

1848
United States receives Nevada and other southwestern land from Mexico by treaty at end of Mexican War.

1850
Utah Territory, which includes most of Nevada, is created.

1861
Nevada Territory is created by Congress.

1865
State school system is established.

1870-81
Value of silver falls, causing many mines to close.

1600   **1700**   **1800**

1492
Christopher Columbus comes to New World.

1607
Capt. John Smith and three ships land on Virginia coast and start first English settlement in New World — Jamestown.

1754–63
French and Indian War.

1773
Boston Tea Party.

1776
Declaration of Independence adopted July 4.

1777
Articles of Confederation adopted by Continental Congress.

1787
U.S. Constitution written.

1812–14
War of 1812.

United States
History At-A-Glance

1900
Silver is discovered at Tonopah; in Ely, copper mines are established.

1902
Gold is discovered at Goldfield, bringing miners back to Nevada.

1907
First federal irrigation project, called the Newlands Irrigation Project, is finished.

1910
Law makes gambling illegal.

1917
World War I creates a demand for supplies, boosting Nevada's mining industry.

1931
Work on Hoover Dam (originally Boulder Dam) is begun.

1931
Gambling is legalized in Nevada; another law is passed to make divorce quick and easy in the state.

1936
Hoover Dam is completed and Lake Mead is created.

1939
World War II stimulates business for Nevada mines; after the war, mining of metal ores declines and mining for nonmetallic minerals takes on greater importance.

1951
Atomic Energy Commission begins testing nuclear weapons in Nevada.

1980
State laws are passed to protect Lake Tahoe from pollution.

1987
Yucca Mountain is named as site of first high-level nuclear waste disposal facility.

1800   **1900**   **2000**

1848
Gold discovered in California draws eighty thousand prospectors in the 1849 Gold Rush.

1861–65
Civil War.

1869
Transcontinental railroad completed.

1917–18
U.S. involvement in World War I.

1929
Stock market crash ushers in Great Depression.

1941–45
U.S. involvement in World War II.

1950–53
U.S. fights in the Korean War.

1964–73
U.S. involvement in Vietnam War.

2000
George W. Bush wins the closest presidential election in history.

2001
A terrorist attack in which four hijacked airliners crash into New York City's World Trade Center, the Pentagon, and farmland in western Pennsylvania leaves thousands dead or injured.

▼ In this 1908 photograph, a New-York-to-Paris-automobile-race contestant, driving a Thomas Flyer car, arrives at Cherry Creek, a mining town.

Festivals and Fun for All

Check web site for exact date and directions.

Basque Festival, Elko

In July, descendants of the Basque people who settled in Nevada gather for a cultural festival. They wear their native costumes and celebrate their heritage with music, games, dancing, and their unique language.
www.elmer.rabbitbrush.com/anacabe/festival.html

Camel Races, Virginia City

In September, this famous Old West town hosts camel races in memory of the days when camels were used in the Nevada desert as pack animals.
www.allcamels.com/storefront/vccr

Clark County Fair, Logandale

This county fair takes place in April and features Western costumes, livestock competitions, games, and regional foods.
www.ccfair.com

Cowboy Poetry Gathering, Elko

In January every year, visitors gather with cattle ranchers, poets, musicians, and enthusiasts of the American West to celebrate this period of American history and the current way of life in the West. The festival includes singing, dancing, poetry readings, exhibits, oral history presentations, and crafts sales and demonstrations.
www.westfolk.org

Desert Inn PGA International Golf Tournament, Las Vegas

This world-famous professional golf event takes place in March, bringing together the best golfers from around the world to compete.
www.golfweb.com/tournaments

Great Reno Balloon Race, Reno

Balloonists from around the world gather in September with their colorful craft to compete in this famous race.
www.renoballoon.com

Jim Butler Days, Tonopah

The town of Tonopah is where Jim Butler discovered one of Nevada's richest deposits of silver ore. Tonopah celebrates its history each year in May. Visitors learn what it was like to live in this boomtown in the early 1900s by attending exhibits and presentations.
www.tonopahnevada.com

Mint 400 Desert Race, Las Vegas
In September, competitors from across the nation gather for buggy racing in the desert.
www.bitd.com

National Championship Air Races and Air Show, Reno
In September, aircraft fill the sky with exciting races and daredevil stunts.
www.airrace.org.

National Finals Rodeo, Las Vegas
This is the Super Bowl of rodeos, bringing together the top competitors in seven events to seek the championship. Country music and Western dress set the mood.
www.prorodeo.com/NFR

Nevada State Fair, Reno
August is the time for this cultural celebration of the state, which features delicious foods, Old West costumes, dancing, singing, games, and agricultural exhibits.
www.nevadastatefair.org

Pony Express Days, Ely
This festival, which takes place in August, features reenactments of the Pony Express and exhibits about this unique chapter of American history.
www.maintour.webpanda.com/white_pine_county

Rhyolite Resurrection Festival, Rhyolite
The ghost town of Rhyolite comes to life as a thriving mining center during this festival in March every year. Food and historical reenactments are some highlights.
www.nevadaweb.com

Shakespeare Festival, Lake Tahoe
Sand Harbor State Park in Lake Tahoe is the home of this festival, which celebrates the Bard's works each year in July and August. Live theater productions of Shakespeare's plays are presented on an outdoor stage with the lake and nearby forests forming a backdrop. Theater summer camps for children are also offered at the site.
www.laketahoeshakespeare.com

Snowfest, North Lake Tahoe
Early March brings the Snowfest, a winter carnival featuring winter sports, foods, craft exhibits, and games.
www.snowfest.org

Winter Carnival, Reno
The University of Nevada at Reno hosts this exciting festival that celebrates the season with winter sports, hearty foods, and arts and crafts exhibits.
www.unr.edu/nevadanews

▲ Top professional cowboys from around the world compete in nine different events at the Reno Rodeo, including the Saddle Bronc.

Books

Clark, Walter Van Tilburg. *The Ox-Bow Incident.* New York: Random House, 1940. This novel, by Nevada's famous writer who grew up in Reno and wrote about the American West, tells the dramatic tale of the lynching of three innocent men who are suspected of cattle rustling.

Gibson, Karen Bush. *Nevada Facts and Symbols.* Mankato, MN: Bridgestone Books, 2001. Learn about the state of Nevada's symbols and the interesting stories behind them.

Marsh, Carole. *Nevada Silly Trivia!* Bath, NC: Gallopade Publishing Group, 1990. Discover intriguing and amazing facts about the Silver State in this collection of facts.

Twain, Mark. *Roughing It.* Berkeley: University of California Press, 1996 (originally published in 1872). This autobiographical account by America's famous writer tells of his adventures in the West, including his stint as a journalist for the Virginia City newspaper.

Young, Bob. *Forged in Silver: The Story of the Comstock Lode.* New York: J. Messner, 1968. This comprehensive history tells the story of the Comstock Lode, Nevada's biggest site of silver ore, which brought thousands of miners to the state in 1859.

Web Sites

▶ Official state web site
www.silver.state.nv.us

▶ Nevada State Symbols
www.50states.com/nevada.htm

▶ Official State of Nevada web site
www.nv.gov

Note: Page numbers in *italics* refer to maps, illustrations, or photographs.